Wisp Of

Smoke

Andrew VanArsdale

Author of *Minority of One*

BRABANT LION

Andrew VanArsdale

Wisp Of Smoke

DEDICATION

In memory of my father

Benjamin Wesley VanArsdale, 1935 – 1999,

and mother

Judith Ann VanArsdale, 1942 – 2015.

"Honor your father and your mother…"

Exodus 20:1

BRABANT LION

"A great fire burns within me, but no one stops to warm themselves at it, and passersby see only a wisp of smoke."

--- Vincent Van Gogh

Andrew VanArsdale

Lilies

I saw lilies this morning.
Red-orange and buttery yellow,
Glistening from an early morning rain.
I was in a hurry when I caught their melody:
A sweet silent chorus of colorful trumpets.
I paused,
Joined in the harmony,
And carried their tune the rest of the day.

Prairie Dancer

The bend and sway of wildflowers in bloom mingles with the wispy, tall grass as I smell the earth-scent in wind on my face…

…and there, in my being, I hear it: the silent, prodding call.

The sparrows dance with an unseen partner as the bees hum their tune causing the butterflies to erupt in laughter…

…and there, in my being I feel it: the peaceful invitation.

The trees on the horizon wave a silent chorus of farewells to the sun's slow retreat as the sky is inflamed with nature's hidden colors…

…and there, in my being it stirs: the spark where life awaits.

The majesty in the handy-work of the keeper of the plains cries out its telltale song to the beat of my awe-struck heart as I bow in joyful acceptance…

…and there, in my being it wells up: mutual joy, a Father's love.

To Conquer the World

I'm told that as a boy Alexander memorized all Achilles' words.
I, however, perused the pages in *Avengers* and *X-men*,
Forged some report cards, too.

I can picture him listening, spellbound,
As The Philosopher read *The Illiad* aloud,
Fire gleaming in his eyes---
I once fell asleep as an old crone rambled about *Beowulf*
(I dreamed of lunch and pretty girls)

Was it because he was tutored by such a man?
Was it innate?
I read *Poetics. Ethics*, too.
And still, I've yet to conquer self,
Let alone the world.

Born To Love

Once born is to love,
And desire thereof,
As into life we sail away.
On the mankind sea,
A ship asearch, we
In the Philos tide do sway
To all the rage
Found with age
Of Eros' stormy blast.
Yet finding shore
We search no more,
Agape harbors at last.

Snow Angel

I watched the glisten in frozen repose,
Of a cherub carved by my stinging toes,
Only to find the distinct impression,
The chilling truth that my expression,
Was, for all my flapping arms unfurled,
Tomorrow gone, unnoticed by the world.

The Difference

A well-worn path a soul did pace,
A gaunt young man with a finty face
With steps intent upon the ground
When soon was heard a familiar sound.

Another soul just then cut in,
Wry with a smile, quick with a grin,
His eye aglint, his mouth to say,
"Greeting friend, going my way?"

The youth, unmoved in step or stride,
His eyes ahead and to neither side,
Swayed by the charm in the voice he heard
Politely returned a single word:

"Hello," it was his mind to speak,
And turned away to onward seek,
When before him leapt the stranger's prance.
The youth then did around him glance.

He sought a way in the undergrowth,
A way he would part them both.
"Join me friend, my dinner to share?"
"No thanks, good sir, I'm going somewhere."

Then the youth pressed ever on,
Again with intentioned expression adon,
As the stranger lost his grin awry,
But he would attempt another try.

(continued)

Before his words again could urge
They met the way two roads diverge,
Where the eye aglint and the flinty face
There did find a parting pace.

And so away his feet did dance,
And behind stood a solemn stance---
The youth gazed on and waved good-bye,
Then chose the road less traveled-by.

Secrets' Secrets

Curious demons stir the mind:
Eve in a garden, Pandora, too---
Like reaching for a bubble,
To know the magical, iridescent orb,
Defying gravity,
Enticingly dancing on air…
But the grasping soul is spat upon,
Leaving a sticky, empty mess.

Cardinal Sins

Two lovers treading a leafy wood
Did dance and play as though they could
Through game their bane affect to flight;
So intent they were in spite
Of truth before their optic sense:
God inflicted Difference.
Amidst their play they found a perch,
On a whited branch among the birch,
Affording the moment to perplex
Both varieties of sex.
The He then cocked his curious crest
And stole a glimpse of Her duller breast
But was also caught by Her wary eye
And thus provoked Her indignant cry!
As She broke flight He turned red
And formed this thought within His head:
"How is it true that She, though not me,
 Could be adorned with modesty?"

Song of Praise

I thought I saw a cherub pink
Upon a hymn once sang in sync
Stop in wonder with surprise
At mortals pausing in their lies,
And then listened so intent,
And marveled at the soulful hint
In sinners breaking from their ways
To offer up a song of praise.

Higher and Bliss

Some say ignorance is equal to bliss,
Some say knowledge is higher.
From what I've learned I know this:
Innocence holds a hint of bliss.
But if I had to further aspire
I've known enough of experience
To say, those wanting a knowledge higher
Have also sense, and should acquire.

Tiger Within

A rustle in the thickets,
Foreboding in the air,
It silences the crickets:
The jungle is aware.
The light above is drowned
By every towering tree,
Barred from reaching ground,
By the leafy canopy,
And beneath in darkness dwells
This creature in the night;
The troubles silence foretells
The coming of his might.
With sinews set to pounce,
And spirit set to soar,
I feel with every ounce
The tiger within me roar!

Seraph Song

I dreamed I joined in lofty song
The Seraphs in their flight,
To view with joy a reverent throng
And chant away in spite
Of angels in their chorused praise
And my thousand eyes could see
Mortals cast their wondrous gaze
To the throne of God below me.

Father's Arms

The moon lies fairer tonight.
Leafy branches are bleached to paleness:
The dappling shadows of limbs are in sway.
Through leaves come flitting whispers,
Silent echoes,
Memories carefully hidden---
My father's house, the child who grew there.
The evening breeze is chilling,
Recalling sleepless nights,
And squandered days,
The coldness of regret.
But the moon peeks ever anew,
And thoughts return now---
The ring on the finger,
The warmth of this robe,
And my Father's warm embrace.

Complacency

I paused to rest and see how great
I'd faired against the whims of fate,
And smiled outright for well I knew
How far I'd come in contrast to
My footprints through the desert sand,
But I discovered in the Promise Land,
Comforts posed a more certain doom
Than struggles in the desert gloom.

Jonathan's Song

A single moment longer!
So precious your embrace,
And see our love is stronger
Through tears upon my face.

And through your mournful cries
I hear the weepy song
Of love without disguise,
A heart where I belong.

But still, a moment longer!
And recall our promise true,
Our Witness will make stronger
The friend I have in you.

Remember well this sad dismay,
For love is prone to grieve,
And wear this warmth each distant day:
The robe that friendships weave.

Morning Mist

What flesh endures the ravage of time,
Shuns not the blink from morn' to dusk?
So spur my thought in their usual way,
As I gaze on a mist that fades by mid-day.
And with such thought works the simples of minds
Whom puts for his labor with little more to find
Than a tiresome ache in the day's late hour,
And a return of spite for his efforts.
Who can watch the radiance of a majestic sunset cloud
Yet savor not it bitter at the coming darkness shroud?
What heart is there alive enjoying the kiss of morning dew,
Upon the veil of night has such mortal thoughts too?
What flesh endures the ravage of time,
Shuns not the blink from morn' to dusk?
So spur my thought in their usual way,
As I gaze on a mist that fades by mid-day.

Elegance

The fragrant kiss of a soft spring breeze,
Silk sheets and polished pearls,
Roses on a grand piano,
And the gentle curve of your smile.

Distant Glimpses

In subtle waves they come to me.
Gently they invade,
Like the tide rising unseen by twilight.
Imbuing themselves in rare, rousing, intrusive incursions---
Visions birth in my soul with a Christ-child radiance.
Sweeping,
Over-washing,
Settling upon my being with the lightness of dew,
Like the caress of mist upon the skin.
A potent surge of divine spirit swells,
I inhale the interloper.
The impregnated air floods my soul,
Like a thousand angelic eddies dancing.
An invasion pierces my fog like an army of light,
Shining distant glimpses through this fleshly darkness,
I see the glisten of divine clarity.
The quiet joy of blissful rapture shuns all mortal thought
As the fellowship brews an unexpected air
Within the subtle waves as they come to me.

Winterscape

Barren, desolate land.
Like some solitary arctic stone I sit alone.
Everywhere, silently descending,
Snowflakes light and settle---
Fragile fragment of frozen memories,
Drifting, drifting…
As I wander my solitary winterscape.
One crystalline thought melts into another
As my world transforms into whited beauty,
Into pure, weightless thoughts of you.

(Untitled)

The sea after a storm,
Sapphires in rain,
The crisp October sky.

Freshly formed obsidian,
Raven-spun silk,
The amorous magic of night.

Dawn't first innocent rays,
A sudden lightening burst,
The coy charm of daffodils.

The silken embrace of rose petals,
A spray of mist in the heat of the day,
The subtle caress of morning dew.

A walk through clouds to the moon and stars,
A favorite dream relived,
A profound mystery longing to be known.

---Your eyes,
   Your hair,
   Your smile.
   Your touch,
   Your kiss.

Pacific Blue

The sand is snowy white,
The sea a somber blue.
The waves roll with steady, dull cadence,
And wash slowly out into salty blue immensity,
A hypnotic rhythm luring towards a deep,
    unknown stillness.
I'm a cloud on the horizon,
And no road has brought me here,
Just a random vapor drifting.
And I shall melt into the deep,
Where there is only blue,
And no memories…
No memories.

Andrew VanArsdale

Angel of March

A fresh wind encompasses me,
Surrounding me in a rushing melee of miraculous mystery,
It hails from majestic heights,
And returns from nether-regions long forgotten---
And at this I tremble.
For it's frailest breeze is a sharpened blade
Poking hidden passions into play,
As though a burst of breath both fragrant and bitter,
A tonic of jasmine and vinegar,
Like a penetrating torrent of fire,
Rousing a vortex magnificently terrifying,
For it rekindles the ashes of a heart once known.
And dreams adrift on a long-soured draft
Rise like a dove before the dawn,
Finding the fresh, flourishing, wind of you.

24

Valkyrie

A sunset is not a single moment,
But moments transcended, an event.
Turning tints and shifting shades glowing---
But then they fade.
The innocent moments fade with the light.
Yet a single moment of light can inspire,
A certain tint can wake glow of desire,
Like a wave set in motion,
Surging, then lost into ocean,
A martyr for a lingering dream,
A faded phantom haunting dreams.

From the edge of shadow I behold you,
Melancholy eyes regard your glowing hue,
And the ebbing dream wakes afresh,
Fading desires are reborn.
The transcended moments are in you embodied,
As if the tides of tints and shades did merge.
A longing glow does rise and surge
Where once was waning it now does wax,
And thus cultivates a continuous climax
Of unrelenting radiant light,
Unfading, innocent light.

Beautiful Night

The wind sweeps out across the plain
    in silent shapeless grace,
And whispers to a towering tree
    which stretches forth an embrace.
The breeze blows in and passes through,
The long leafy limbs whose moon-blanched hue,
In a flightless flurry with a flowing bend and sway,
Waves a belated farewell to a long-since faded day.
And the weight of thought is lifted,
    the mind drifts light and free,
As the wood becomes the wind
    and the wind becomes the tree.
For I am now the branches and I'm reaching out to you,
As your grace saturates my soul and passes softly through,
And I am in you and you are in me
    as our mingled souls embrace,
And our love is a night of beauty
    transcending time and space.

Lingering Thought

Some thoughts longingly linger,
Some pass forgotten in time.
Some moments are the bringer
Of a thousand thoughts sublime.
For I find this mind does sometimes dwell
On what it can't let go,
And though I try to stop and quell,
Instead do embrace and flow,
And return again to capture
A moment that did seem
Like sweet angelic rapture,
A divinely recurrent dream.
And I weakly smile in conflicted bliss
Upon realizing to be true,
To my surprise, what I miss
Is that moment spent with you.

Andrew VanArsdale

Unexpected Depth

Rock resists ready removal,
Earthly flesh fights foolishly.
And yet the grieving ground gives way,
Weary weak walls fall back,
Swayed to submit stone-sealed secrets,
And a dreaded dampness trickles into the terrible darkness.
An unfettered flow meanders in,
Vanquishing the vile void as does blood in a wound.
And the heart of the cold cavity is cleverly transformed,
For in the uninvited vacancy
Is found unexpected depth.

Doe of the Morning

In the early hours of twilight just before the dawn,
In the brush there is the stirring of a fragile little fawn.
Though stars as yet glimmer and moon still holds high,
It makes to steal a drink from the quiet brook nearby.
Cautiously from the forest's edge it slowly makes its way,
For to drink it must be vulnerable to many beasts of prey.
Drinking it's fill it finds a soothing, refreshing balm,
As the water renews life and the thirsting soul is calm.
Though the day will bring much danger, still it is blessed
By the flow of living water, bringing peace to life and rest.

Andrew VanArsdale

Luther's Grave

Walking one eve during summer's last
I noticed an archaic cemetery I passed,
So I strolled through where the dead did lay
Where I encountered a peculiar stone in my way.
Then so suddenly it gave me a start,
The ground trembled and broke apart!
From the grave below I saw arise
A horrid thing with rotted eyes!
I gasped in amazement and did stare
At this hideous sight before me there.
"Good sir," said he, "what is the year,
  Or could you tell me how long I've been here?"
"T'is two thousand-nine since the birth of our Lord
  Who was killed years alter by an angry hoard.
  To the length of your stay I know not,
  How is it you cam to so grim a spot?"
Brushing a maggot from his chin,
Ha gave what seemed a sociable grin.
"Friend," he croaked in a scratchy voice,
  "I'm here by necessity, not by choice.
  I've gone the way of Everyman,
  To escape this fate are none who can."
"If this be so then how can there be
  This priestly carcass before me I see?"
"Why friend, I tell you it was not enough
  To turn in my grave and become ashen stuff.
  While with worms there I did rotting lie
  The stones rang out a compelling cry!
  So I crawled from this plot with this to give:
  The spirit if Tetzel yet does live!
  False religion yet lurks, that wicked beast,

(continued)

On your soul, too, it longs to feast!
This new faith is strangely odd,
It has no sanctuary nor a god.
It is faith in no faith, I'm telling you true,
 Now guard yourself before lightening gets you!
 Take up your shield and your spirit sword,
 Nail a new thesis to another board!
 Address your nobility, every ruler and prince,
 Stand for true faith and a clear conscience."
Then as I stood among his stench and smell,
My conscience indeed began to swell.
"Friend," I said, "I give you my word,
 That which you say, my heart has heard."
The carcass' breath seemed to give as he passed
And I continued my walk during summer's last.

Walking Down Poplar Street

Broken sidewalks.
Tiny, tattered brown shack,
Scattered grass blades, mostly dirt---
Deep waters stir, questions of truth or dream;
Intriguingly obscure.

Zero to four,
Smallest, humble beginning,
Skinny, blond, blue   ---strange.

The kind candy woman,
Hide and seek,
No shoes,
Few toys   ---the neighbors murdered mom.

Nothing like I remember.

Do Not Destroy

Do not destroy the innocence of a child,
    the trust,
    the smile.
And take pains to spare the daffodil patch when
    plowing.
And if a neighbor falls, reach to warm their crushed
    spirit.
The bite of cruel, destructive winds knows no creed,
    nor age,
    nor reason,
    nor purpose...

So do not destroy a mother's laughter,
    a young man's dreams,
    an infant's blissful sleep.
Allow the Monarch to slowly exercise and abruptly
    flutter.
Take time to cheer a tearful freckled face,
    tickle a wooly-worm,
    and make an old man smile.

Andrew VanArsdale

A Dove On Distant Oaks

In early stillness among morning dew,
Where fog still lingers though night is through,
The quiet breaks to the telltale cry
Of a gentle dove in some oaks nearby.

From slumber I stir to face the day
And brush the dew in my eyes away,
Sleepily recalling the phantoms of dream
And the intrigue of how real they often seem.

In a motionless moment I reflectively listen:
The singsong dove, the dew's telling glisten,
And there I find a compelling thought
Of joys the morning often brought.

In slumber a man lives in desperate plight,
As there lies no hope in the raven of night.
Though in bliss one swells in ignorant sleep,
In the flights of dream is no truth to keep.

When the dawn rears forth dispelling the dark,
And the morning dove lights on the oaken bark
The spirit awaks in the light of truth,
The revealing presence of a new day's youth.

Welcome is the morning and dove's abrupt flutter
Which come to open the spirit's dark shutter
And the addled shadow the light now chokes
As the morning dove sings from the distant oaks.

Song

Spirit drifting, mysteriously aflow,
Unaware of raptured bliss:
A strange new note,
Or familiar lyric---
Drowning the song of self.
Melodic charm conducts the thoughts:
Memory's tune relived.
The harmony strikes a cord of truth,
As I hear my soul join in.

Little Girls and Daisies

Walking through the field of daisies
I've found they're really very kind:
They bow, blow a kiss on the breeze,
And whisper secrets to the butterfly and bee.

And in the smile of little girl's shy, freckled face
There's a silly giggle,
A tongue waggling through a toothless gap,
And inescapably touching innocence.

But then there's the sunset, the rainbow, the autumn leaves.
The incoherent crickets' chorus
On a star-lit summer's eve,
And the butterfly's dance to the bee's low drone.

There's no burden in the careless sway of trees,
Sparrows playing in the sky,
Daisies blowing a kiss on the breeze,
Or in a little girl's freckle-faced smile.

Walking With My Grandfather
(Dover Revisited)

We smiled and laughed as we went.
I kicked bare toes into the cooling sand
And tugged at the wrinkled hand engulfing mine.
The cliff and the sea hemmed us in,
Caught where two worlds collide.
He suddenly paused in silence;
I saw salt , snow, or something on the cliff's side.
So small did I feel, yet even smaller
As he stooped and clutched my shoulders,
"Listen!" he pleaded,
I heard only the tide's grating roar.
Her pursed his lips and seemed so sad,
"The sea always remains unmoved," he whispered.
I nodded and we continued on.
The cliff seemed somehow less imposing,
And the sea now beckoned, alluring.
We crossed the span of that darkling plain,
I felt strangely at peace.

Snow Blanket

The fields lie quietly sleeping.
Neatly tucked under blanketing snow,
Rolling hills are their cradle.
Across the plain whips the wind;
Drowsy pines are roused:
"Behold," comes a whisper,
"Where now lies the weary, waiting soil?"
The pines sway an ignorant shrug
And considered that perhaps it's covered.
"Correct," echoes over the white winter earth,
"And peaceful is it's rest."
They tossed a tuft of snow to the breeze,
"And the babble in the brook?"
"Bubbling," calls the wind,
"Wet are it's wanting rocks."
"Why?" ponders the pines.

Stillness…

The willing wind rests in silence,
The swaying pines do not shrug,
And in all the valley is no sound.
The heavens declare the quiet song,
The skies proclaim their resounding answer,
Hills and fields glint and twinkle---
A choir of exaltation…

The wind prods the pines playfully,
Again they bow in agreement,
"But of course," they remark,
"How could we forget?"

Beatific

Subtly comes the moment
When, in a smiley grin or glance,
We catch a fleeting glimpse, a hint
In an action done by chance,
And view within the mortal flesh
An amazing wealth of grace,
To wonder how God did enmesh
His image with Time and Space.

The Sleeper and the Stallion

"Balance," he told me, "nothing to excess,"
"As your passions drive you, Prudence, too, will bless."
I pondered thereafter the wisdom of his word,
And gave a thoughtful ear to all that I had heard.

"The sleeper," I then asked, "is this not one so wise?
 Prudence conduct him safely, from Vice he hides his eyes."

"Though the Sleeper does so dream of joy and ideal bliss,
 Of a prudent peaceful life and a lover's tender kiss,
 Therein is only apathy, a dull slothful hand,
 He has no heart to face his trials, no spirit for the grand.
 Though he shows restraint, no passion there does bless,
 And so, in dream, he's a dying soul, sleeping to excess!"

"The Stallion then," I replied, "surely there would wisdom be!"
 His countenance is so vital, his spirit strong and free!"

"Listen well, my friend, what I speak is true,
 Though he be so fierce, there wisdom never knew.
 I watched as flames did blow with wind from tree to tree
 And with the quickness it had com brought death for all to see.
 The Stallion, full of fire, with vigor to expend,
 Is blown and tossed as a reckless leaf to meet a hasty end.
 A life where passions burn without restraint to bless
 Is a heart that has no balance, ever given to excess."

"Tell me then," I pleaded, "who is wise or true?
 And how may I grow likewise? What am I to do?"
My heart, vexed and wrenched, heard his solemn voice express,
"Balance," he said smiling, "and nothing to excess."

Empty Words of Wanda

She showed me around,
Intro's and the grand tour,
Her frequent laughter was infectious…

Lou Gehrig's they said,
"So sad",
I had a sad thought, too,
Then went back to work.

"Married late, two years ago,
  Highschool sweetheart," they said.
I wonder how she feels?
Her husband?

I saw her six months later.
She clashed against the wheelchair,
Like a rainbow in a prison cell.
She smiled upward desperately, bravely:
Our mutual thought of my first day,
(Her restrained tears pleaded for help)
I just kept thinking of her former laughter.

I asked God to forgive my apathy,
But He still haunts me with her laughter.

Andrew VanArsdale

Chopin On Irvine Street

Our bubble environment sped comfortably,
As the refined melody danced
And the air-conditioned breeze was controlled.
A single turn transitioned from suburb to Irvine Street:
Unkempt rows of tiny shacks,
Black women with babies squinting in the heat---
The music flowed sweetly, my soul drifted to bliss,
Like practiced ballet amidst untamed jungle.
Oblivious, we slowed at the tracks:
Staring, squinting black men,
Their radio blared and broke our bubble---
Seeming noise to our Chopin.
I gazed at his dark flesh in the sun,
One spoke and smiled bright white,
Another laughed heartily.
I smiled, too,
But then drifted back to bliss.

The Owl

On a murky eve darkened by cloud,
The starless heavens draped in a shroud
Played hide and seek with the moon's dull light,
And upon the earth was untimely night.

In the humid breeze walked a single soul,
Alone in the dark, away he stole,
To the lonesome woods where lovers play
In the happier hours in the noon of the day.

A familiar log there found his perch,
Near gnarled trees mingled with birch
And a tearful wail filled the air
With the mournful cry of a heart in despair.

"Like this darkness here in the night
  Is this searching soul hidden from light,
  As this meaningless life with a plague in the heart
  Haunts this existence and tears me apart!"

"Here shall I rest until I find
  Hope or death---life must be defined!"
Then, with surprise from the midnight blue,
There spoke a serious, somber "Who?"

The lad, aghast, in shock and dismay,
Turned with a jerk to the sober display
Of gleaming eyes of fiery gold,
As he shook and trembled under terror's hold.

Andrew VanArsdale

(continued)

"Adam's the name," he stuttered in fear,
"What brings your presence to draw so near?"
Silence ensued the questioned air
As he sat beneath the dark horned glare.

"Who?" it came back, unmoved or stirred,
Silhouetting grimly sat the hulking bird.
The boy sat still and reflectively thought,
"'Who?' he asks this soul distraught?"

"What shall I say to answer him true?
  Fortune? Fame? Perhaps Romance, too?
  Oh, Christ! I don't know the answer at all!
Silent became the stranger, no longer to call.

ABOUT THE AUTHOR

Andrew VanArsdale is a native of central Kentucky. He spent his youth wandering the expansive farm fields near his home where the seeds of admiration for natural wonders were planted. Though a day-dreaming underachiever during his school years, he demonstrated an aptitude for creativity, especially in writing. This carried over into his college years at Eastern Kentucky University, where he wrote extensive essays and research papers in philosophy and religion. During this time his passive church interest was transformed into an earnest faith, as the day-dreaming kid wandering farm fields learned to examine the wonders of creation, and he formally majored in both Philosophy and Religion. Becoming an unlikely disciplined student, Andrew received the Department Award for Religious Studies. The advent of a more disciplined life led to his long-time penchant for scribbling rhymes blossoming into thoughtful poems acknowledging the natural beauty of the world, comments of Christian faith, and ponderings on human nature. This would later become the raw material for his first book, *Wisp of Smoke*. Andrew is an avid reader and has found lasting literary influence in such notable fiction writers as O'Conner, Frost, and Dostoevsky, among others.

Nemo vir est qui mundum non reddat meliorem